This book belongs to:

The
SAME SUN
WAS in the SKY

BY DENISE WEBB

ILLUSTRATED BY WALTER PORTER

Northland Publishing

The paintings in this book were done in watercolor on Crescent cold press illustration board
The display type was set in Trajan and Recklman Solid
The text type was set in Deepdene
Composition by Northland Publishing
Designed by Trina Stahl
Edited by Kathryn Wilder
Production supervised by Lisa Brownfield
Manufactured in Hong Kong by Regent Publishing Services

FIRST EDITION

ISBN 0-87358-602-6
Library of Congress Catalog Card Number 94-40959
Cataloging-in-Publication Data
Webb, Denise, 1951-
The same sun was in the sky / by Denise Webb ; illustrated by Walter Porter. — 1st ed.
p. cm.
Summary : A boy and his grandfather go hiking in the Arizona desert,
where they observe the many rock carvings and imagine the lives of the
Hohokam people who lived there in ancient times.
ISBN 0-87358-602-6 : $14.95
1. Hohokam culture—Juvenile fiction. [1. Hohokam culture—Fiction. 2. Indians of North
America—Southwest, New—Antiquities—Fiction. 3. Grandfathers—Fiction.]
I. Porter, Walter, ill. II. Title.
PZ7.W367Sam 1994
[Fic]—dc20   94-40959

0546/7.5M/3-95

In memory of my father, George Petty, the "Grandpa" in our family;
and with thanks to my mother, Sylvia McMullin, and to Joseph Boudreaux,
for believing in me; and to Linda Gregonis for her expert advice on the ways
of the Hohokam.

—D. W.

To my wife, Betsy, and my children, Nicholas, Alexandra, and Philip:
Thank you for putting up with me throughout this very long but
rewarding project.

—W. P.

TODAY MY GRANDFATHER has brought me to our special place in the desert. It's a hill covered with big rocks. On the rocks are drawings made by people hundreds, maybe thousands of years ago. These drawings weren't painted on, they were pecked into the rocks with sharp pieces of hard stone.

I like climbing on the rocks and finding as many pictures as I can. I try to figure out what they are. There are a lot of pictures that look like the sun. Some pictures are spirals, like snakes coiled up ready to strike.

There is one picture of a man standing by a maze. I like to follow the path into the middle.

There are lots of pictures of animals with horns.

"Those are bighorn sheep," says Grandpa. "They were hunted by the people who lived here."

One picture reminds me of a snake slithering back and forth over the ground, and one looks like a man holding up the sky.

There are some pictures that don't remind me of anything.

"Maybe they're just nice designs," says Grandpa, "or maybe they meant something to the people who drew them. They could have been clan symbols, which is like writing your last name."

"What do you call these drawings, Grandpa?" I ask, because I always forget the name.

"They're called petroglyphs," he answers, "which means rock carvings. The rocks on this hill are the best kind for making petroglyphs. See how they have a dark outer layer," he says, bending down to one of the rocks, "but they're lighter-colored underneath."

"So when you peck into the dark layer, the light color shows up and makes the picture stand out," I say, pleased with myself for figuring it out.

"That's right," says Grandpa. I can tell he's proud of me. "The people who made these pictures used sharp, hard stones to peck at the rocks, like a woodpecker pecks at a tree. They would peck one mark after another until all the marks joined together into a picture or a design."

Grandpa has told me a lot about the people who made these drawings. He says it's important to remember those who came before us.

"We call these people the Hohokam," Grandpa says. "They lived for over a thousand years in this desert, up until five hundred years ago. They were a part of the desert, just like the snake and the lizard and the saguaro cactus. Everything they needed came from their neighbors, the plants and animals of the desert."

As Grandpa talks I can almost see these people. I imagine them coming up the hill on the same path we took to get to the top. They are dark skinned, with long, straight hair. They wear only sandals, and a cloth around their middle.

"Their clothes were made from the cotton they grew in their fields and made into cloth," says Grandpa, "and their sandals were made by weaving together the dried leaves of the yucca plant."

"Didn't they get cold in the winter?" I ask.

"They made warm clothes from animal skins," says Grandpa.

Maybe, I think, maybe a Hohokam boy once sat in the same spot I'm sitting in now. He probably looked at the drawings on the rocks, too. But he knew who put them there and what they meant. Maybe he even pecked a picture into the rocks himself.

The same sun was in the sky then. Maybe he saw the sun low in the sky like it is now, with its rays shooting out in all directions. Maybe he drew a picture of it right here.

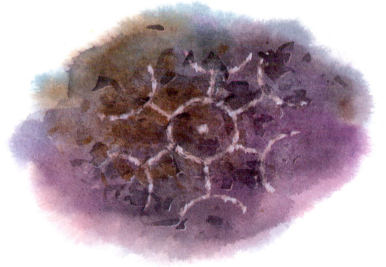

"Why did the Hohokam people come to this spot?" I ask. "Why did they draw all these pictures here?"

"No one really knows," says Grandpa, "but if we're good detectives, we might be able to figure out some possible reasons. Let's look at the clues around us. This hill we're on was pretty easy for us to climb, but from the top we can see in all directions."

"We sure can," I say, as I slowly twirl around in a circle.

"With such a good view, we could easily see anyone else coming our way," says Grandpa. "This might have been a good, safe place for travelers to stop and rest and leave their clan symbols on the rocks. Traders might have stopped here, too, on the way to trade for shells from the ocean. The Hohokam made jewelry by etching pictures on seashells. Now, look around you—what do you see?"

"Well," I answer, "I see the desert all around us, and lots of saguaro cactus."

"Yes," says Grandpa, as he finds a good rock to sit on under a palo verde tree. "Those saguaros grow more than just funny-looking arms. Every summer they grow fruit up on top of their branches that is good to eat. The Hohokam might have come here to harvest the saguaro fruit."

"How did they get the fruit down?" I ask. "Those saguaros are too tall and too prickly to climb."

"Well, they might have done what the Tohono O'odham tribe still does today. They use long poles made from the ribs of dead saguaros. They knock the fruit off the saguaro with a pole and catch it when it falls," says Grandpa, swinging an imaginary stick. "The Hohokam could see lots of things to eat in this desert, like the fruit on that prickly pear cactus, or the weeds growing in the wash. This palo verde tree grows beans that can be eaten, and so does the mesquite tree."

I think about the Hohokam boy. I can see him at the bottom of a giant saguaro, catching fruit in a basket as his mother knocks it down with her pole, or helping to pick the long bean pods hanging on the mesquite tree.

"They might have camped near this hill during the harvest," says Grandpa, "and maybe they drew pictures on the rocks just for the fun of it, or as their artwork. They might have liked to draw as much as you do."

"I guess they didn't have any paper," I say.

"No, they didn't. Now," says Grandpa, turning around on his rock, "look behind us at the low mountains. In those mountains lives another important food for the Hohokam, the bighorn sheep. The people might have come here when they were hunting the sheep. They might have carved the pictures of the sheep on the rocks for good luck in their hunting, or to make a record of the sheep they killed."

I think about the Hohokam boy again. Maybe he helped the older boys and men when they shot an animal with their bows and arrows. Maybe he just helped by catching mice and lizards. Grandpa says they ate those, too.

"Now look in front of us at the sunset," says Grandpa, "and at all the sun pictures on the rocks. The sun was very important to the Hohokam. They knew they needed the sun to survive, and they might have considered it to be a god. Maybe this was a special place for ceremonies for their god, the sun. Like a church would be for you."

"It's a nice place for a church, isn't it, Grandpa?" I say.

"Yes," he says quietly, and we sit for awhile not saying anything, just watching the sunset.

Then I ask, "Did they live near here, Grandpa?"

"Some of them lived in the same place our city is now," he answers. "Remember the dry riverbed we walk down sometimes?"

"Yes," I say. "Once it had water in it after it rained."

"That's the one," says Grandpa, putting his arm around my shoulder. "It's dry now because our city pumps the water from underground and doesn't leave any for the river. But once that river flowed all the time, and there was a big Hohokam village right next to it."

"What happened to the village?" I ask.

"Parts of it are still there, underneath our city. Sometimes when people build new buildings, they come across the ruins of Hohokam houses, and they even find some of their things, like bits of pottery or the weapons and tools they made of rock."

"What did their houses look like?" I ask.

"The Hohokam dug into the ground to make the floor of the house." Grandpa shows this to me by digging into the ground with a stick. "Then they built over the sunken-in part with wood and brush, and covered it with mud."

"I bet the children helped put the mud on," I say.

"Probably," Grandpa says. "The houses were just one room where everyone slept. The cooking was done outside, and people sat outside to sew or make their pottery and tools."

"Where did they go to the bathroom?" I ask. Grandpa will answer anything I want to know.

"They probably had a place to go outside, away from the buildings," says Grandpa, smiling. "They had no plumbing for things like toilets and sinks."

"Maybe they took baths in the river," I say. I can see the Hohokam boy splashing with his friends in the water.

"Yes," says Grandpa. "They used the river for their drinking water, too, and they dug canals to get the water from the river to their crops of corn, squash, and beans, or they planted right near the river in the floodplain." Now Grandpa is drawing long canals with his stick. "They grew what food they could, and went out into the desert to get the rest."

"But they couldn't drive here like we did, could they, Grandpa?" I say.

"No, there were no cars then, no wagons; they didn't even have horses to ride. The Hohokam walked wherever they went, and carried the things they needed on their backs. When they moved through the desert they heard the sound of the wind in the palo verde trees, or the rustle of a lizard darting through a bush. There was nothing else. Not like now, when we can hear the sounds of cars going by on the highway and jet planes overhead."

In my mind I can see the people walking through the desert, and I see the boy again, but he's not walking quietly, he's laughing and running. "Maybe the kids chased after horned toads and lizards when they walked, or maybe they played tag," I say.

"Maybe," says Grandpa.

The sun goes down behind the mountains, and
Grandpa builds a fire in the fire pit. He says we
can stay for a little while. As I watch the stars
coming out in the sky all around us, I draw pictures
in the sand with a stick, pictures like I saw on the rocks
today. I imagine the Hohokam boy sitting beside me,
drawing the same pictures. Maybe he had a grandpa who
told him stories about the ones who came before them.

"Grandpa," I say, "someday we'll be the ones who came before."

"Yes," says Grandpa. "Someday some grandpa might be telling his grandson about a thousand years ago in the twentieth century, when people drove cars and watched television. Maybe they'll dig up the ruins of your house and find some of your toys, and try to figure out what they are."

I try to imagine the boy in the future, and I see him
landing on this same hill in his rocket car, standing on
the same rocks I stood on today, under the same sun.
He'll look at the pictures on the rocks, too, if they're still
here. As I think about that boy from the future, I wonder
if the Hohokam boy ever tried to imagine me.

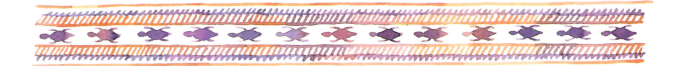

AUTHOR'S NOTE

THE HOHOKAM LIVED in southern Arizona from about 300 to 1500 A.D. They may have come to Arizona from Mexico, or they may have developed out of an earlier group of desert dwellers called Archaic people, who were hunters and gatherers. Many Hohokam settled along the Salt and Gila rivers, and in other parts of the Sonoran Desert. Hohokam settlements have also been found as far north as Flagstaff, Arizona, and as far south as the Mexican border. The Hohokam boy in this story lived along the Santa Cruz River in the same place where the city of Tucson now lies. There were about two hundred people in his village, and there were several other villages nearby.

The Hohokam discovered ways to make life in the desert easier. Because they could bring water to their crops through irrigation, they were able to settle into permanent villages and become farmers. They did not have to keep moving in search of food like earlier groups of desert people. Their pit houses were well built for life in the desert. The sunken floor provided extra cooling in the summer and heating in the winter. The Hohokam made pottery from clay found in desert washes and painted it with red paint on tan or brown backgrounds.

Archaeologists do not know for sure what type of clothing the Hohokam wore, but they do know that the Hohokam wore shell and stone jewelry. (Shell, stone, and pottery last for hundreds of years, whereas cloth does not.) They were the first people in the Americas to etch pictures onto seashells. Hohokam traders traveled far to trade for shells from the ocean, copper bells from Mexico, and turquoise and serpentine from lands to the north and west.

Ceremonies were important in the lives of the Hohokam. Archaeologists have found large, flat-topped mounds of earth at the sites of Hohokam villages that may have been used for dancing. Hohokam pottery shows dancers holding hands, probably dancing in a circle. Ceremonial ball games may have taken place in large oval courts found dug into the earth.

The Hohokam tribes grew and changed over the years as they came into contact with other groups of people. By 1300, the Hohokam began building large, multistoried adobe buildings similar to those made by people in northern Mexico. Around 1500, the Hohokam abandoned the big houses. Archaeologists cannot be sure what happened to them after that, which has caused some people to say that they "mysteriously disappeared." However, it's likely that many Hohokam moved away because of flooding and drought, overpopulation, and maybe fighting and wars. It is also possible that the Hohokam didn't leave at all, and that they are the ancestors of modern-day Pima and Tohono O'odham (Papago) tribes.

Petroglyphs like those the boy and his grandfather found in the story can be found all over the world, made by many different groups of people. When visiting petroglyphs, it is important to remember a few things that will help save them for future generations to enjoy. First, you must never remove the rocks that the petroglyphs are carved on. It is also important not to walk on them, touch them, or make rubbings from them, which could wear them away. Making marks on or near them could damage them, as well. If you want to copy the designs, draw them in the sand or on a piece of paper.

Here is a good motto to follow in any place of beauty we want to preserve for the future: Take only pictures, and leave only footprints. That way, the boy in the rocket car may not only find signs of you having lived here, but of the Hohokam people, too. And he will know that the same sun was in the sky then.